Date: 2/1/12

J 598.418 BOD
Bodden, Valerie.
Swans /

Published by Creative Education
P.O. Box 227, Mankato, Minnesota 56002
Creative Education is an imprint of
The Creative Company
www.thecreativecompany.us

Design and production by The Design Lab
Art direction by Rita Marshall
Printed by Corporate Graphics
in the United States of America

Photographs by Getty Images (Jose Asel/Auora,
Jeff Foott, Eastcott Momatiuk, Michael S. Quinton),
iStockphoto (Richard Bowden, Eric Isselee, Laure
Neish, Vladimirs Prusakovs, Martin Sach, Sally Scott,
Olga Solavei, Tammy Wolfe)

Library of Congress Cataloging-in-Publication Data
Bodden, Valerie.
Swans / by Valerie Bodden.
p. cm. — (Amazing animals)
Includes bibliographical references and index.
ISBN 978-1-58341-719-5
1. Swans—Juvenile literature. I. Title.

QL696.A52B63 2009
598.4'18—dc22   2007051589

CPSIA: 121510 PO1414
9 8 7 6 5 4

AMAZING ANIMALS

SWANS

BY VALERIE BODDEN

CREATIVE EDUCATION

Swans are big birds. There are seven kinds of swans in the world. All of them are good at flying and swimming.

Swans have long necks and big beaks

Swans are covered with feathers. Most swans have white feathers. But some swans have black feathers. Swans have long necks. They have long wings, too.

Swans grow long feathers
as they get older

Swans are some of the biggest birds that can fly. Some swans weigh more than 20 pounds (9 kg). They can be as tall as a second-grader. Even though they are big birds, swans can fly fast. Some can fly as fast as a car drives on the highway!

Swans look extra big when they spread their wings

*Some swans live in cold
areas for part of the year*

Swans like to live close to water. Some swans live in the **Arctic** in the summer. In the fall, these swans **migrate**. They fly to where it is warmer.

Arctic an area at the top of Earth where no trees grow

migrate move to a new home in another area

Swans like to eat plants that grow underwater. Some swans eat fish, too. Sometimes swans eat plants from farmers' fields.

Swans find most of their food in shallow water

Swans watch over their eggs to keep them safe

Mother swans lay eggs. They sit on the eggs to keep them warm. After a while, the eggs **hatch**. The young swans can swim almost right away. They learn to fly after one or two months. Wild swans can live for more than 25 years.

hatch break open

*These swans form a heart
shape with their necks*

Swans spend part of their day resting on land. They spend some of the day swimming, too. They paddle their **webbed feet** to move around in the water. They stick their heads under the water to pull up plants to eat.

webbed feet feet with toes that are joined together by pieces of skin

In the fall and spring, most swans spend a lot of time flying. They migrate to their new homes. They might make sounds as they fly. Some swans make "hoo-hoo" sounds. Other swans sound like a trumpet.

Swans may fly a long way when they migrate

Lots of people like to look at swans. Some people go to zoos to see swans. Other people go to places where swans live in the wild. Swans are some of the prettiest birds in the world!

Swans usually like to be around other swans

A *Swan Story*

Why are some swans black? People on the **continent** of Australia used to tell a story about this. They said that two white swans once rested on a lake. But big hawks lived on the lake. The hawks pulled out the swans' feathers. Some crows felt sorry for the swans. They gave the swans some of their black feathers to wear. From then on, swans in Australia had black feathers!

continent one of Earth's seven big pieces of land

Read More

Cooper, Jason. *Trumpeter Swan*. Vero Beach, Fla.: Rourke, 1997.

Wexo, John Bonnett. *Ducks, Geese & Swans*. San Diego, Calif.: Wildlife Education, 1998.

Web Sites

A Kid's Heart: Swans
http://akidsheart.com/animals/birds/swans.htm
This site has swan facts, activities, and coloring pages.

Swans in a Pond
http://www.uptoten.com/kids/boowakwala-coloring-coloring-landscape.html
This site has a swan coloring activity.

Index

SWANS

24